WORKBOOK

FOR

UNREASONABLE

HOSPITALITY

(A Guide to Will Guidara's Book)

The Effective Guide to
Harnessing the Power of
Giving People More than
They Expect

<u>HOW TO USE THIS</u>
<u>WORKBOOK</u>

- Have a deep and sincere desire to do the things that is recommended here.

- Ponder upon and meditate on the food for thought, reflecting on how they relate to you, what you're advised to do and how to go about doing them.

- In the note section, write down important decisions you've made, relating to the things you've learnt.

- Don't discard this book when you're done with the 7 – Days Program. Instead, always have it in mind, never failing to return when you appear to be deviating.

- Make this a lifestyle. You'd find out that there was far more to gain in the main book through using this practical guide.

- Never assume that the lessons here are difficult and impossible to achieve, they're realistic and made easy for you.

- **Follow the daily outline religiously, don't jump days or prioritize one activity over the other.**

- Everything outlined here is important for you, don't neglect any.

- We recommend that you spread love and help with this workbook, give people whom you feel would need it. It could go a long way.

ALL THE BEST AS YOU
VENTURE INTO THIS.....

1st DAY

FOOD FOR THOUGHT

Becoming generous starts from your ability to understand the benefits of generosity. The sun does not shine for itself; you must not live solely by yourself.

TASK FOR THIS DAY

Understand that good peace and happiness comes from generosity. It is one of the most effective means of building love, learn this today.

<u>KEEP THIS TO HEART...</u>

Contrary to what many people think,
there are numerous self-benefits
attached to being generous.

IMPORTANT REFLECTIONS (NOTES)

_____

_____

_____

_____

_____

_____

_____

_____

_____

_____

_____

_____

_____

_____

_____

_____

_____

_____

_____

_____

_____

_____

_____

_____

_____

_____

_____

PIN THIS!

Put a smile on people's face with the things you were blessed with.

2nd DAY

FOOD FOR THOUGHT

Your ability to be grateful for the things you have is proven to influence your level of generosity. People who appreciate the gifts of this life hardly become misers.

TASK FOR THIS DAY

Start being thankful and expressing gratitude for the things you have. By this way, you'd be able to be more generous.

<u>KEEP THIS TO HEART...</u>

Count your blessings, smile and be
happy for the gift of them.

IMPORTANT REFLECTIONS (NOTES)

_____
_____
_____
_____
_____
_____
_____
_____
_____
_____
_____
_____
_____
_____
_____

_____

_____

_____

_____

_____

_____

_____

_____

_____

_____

_____

PIN THIS!

Be happy and reap the love and peace
of this life.

3rd DAY

FOOD FOR THOUGHT

It's never easy to swing suddenly and entirely into full blown generosity. It's usually a painful and gradual process.

TASK FOR THIS DAY

If you have never given away money, start this by giving away as little as $1. The most important thing is to start somewhere, start small and grow from it.

<u>KEEP THIS TO HEART...</u>

The universe has a way of returning to givers 10x what they give to others.

<u>IMPORTANT REFLECTIONS (NOTES)</u>

_____

_____

_____

_____

_____

_____

_____

_____

_____

_____

_____

_____

_____

_____

_____

_____

_____

_____

_____

_____

_____

_____

_____

_____

_____

<u>PIN THIS!</u>

**You adjust to the pain of generosity
by starting small.**

4th DAY

FOOD FOR THOUGHT

Making your first expense an act of giving is a very good practice for becoming generous.

TASK FOR THIS DAY

When you receive your next paycheck, make your first chunk of expense to be for generosity.

KEEP THIS TO HEART...

When you give as among your first
expense, you'd be less likely to feel
pain and more acquainted to
becoming used to it.

IMPORTANT REFLECTIONS (NOTES)

_____

_____

_____

_____

_____

_____

_____

_____

_____

_____

_____

_____

_____

_____

_____

_____

_____

_____

_____

_____

_____

_____

_____

_____

_____

_____

_____

PIN THIS!

Give from the new joy of receiving.

5th DAY

FOOD FOR THOUGHT

Another beautiful style of generosity is your ability to divert one specific expense to charity.

TASK FOR THIS DAY

Choose a part of your expense to sacrifice and give the returns to charity.

KEEP THIS TO HEART...

Giving is a very beautiful way of receiving blessings. Don't hesitate to give.

IMPORTANT
REFLECTIONS (NOTES)

_____

_____

_____

_____

_____

_____

_____

_____

_____

_____

_____

_____

__PIN THIS!__

Don't eat every single thing, sacrifice
some for charity.

6th DAY

FOOD FOR THOUGHT

Finding out your passion and supporting it with generous donations is another beautiful way of building the spirit of generosity.

TASK FOR THIS DAY

Find out something that you enjoy; sports, swimming, or any good social event. Support it generously, build your giving spirit from this.

KEEP THIS TO HEART...

Supporting your passion hits
difference, it does not pain so much.

IMPORTANT
REFLECTIONS (NOTES)

_____

_____

_____

_____

_____

_____

_____

_____

_____

_____

_____

_____

<u>PIN THIS!</u>

Fuel your passion!

36

7th DAY

FOOD FOR THOUGHT

You get to understand people better when you spend more time with them. Don't judge a person from far, it's not wise or nice.

TASK FOR THIS DAY

Start relating better with people in need, understand their pain and sorrow. This will condition you better to help more.

<u>KEEP THIS TO HEART...</u>

Never judge a book by its cover. That "proud" person might be battling depression.

<u>IMPORTANT REFLECTIONS (NOTES)</u>

_____

_____

_____

_____

_____

_____

_____

_____

_____

_____

_____

<u>PIN THIS!</u>

Meet with more people, socialize better!

CONGRATULATIONS!

YOU MADE IT TO THE END OF THE 7 DAYS PROGRAM.

IMBIBE THE THINGS YOU'VE LEARNT AS A LIFESTYLE!

Made in United States
Troutdale, OR
10/03/2024

23392778R00030